Bryan Owen was born in Whitstable, England in 1947. After nearly twenty years teaching English and drama including two years as a volunteer on an American Lutheran mission station in Papua New Guinea he was ordained into the ministry of the Anglican (Episcopal) Church and served in parishes in both Scotland and England. He has travelled widely and is a frequent visitor to the United States and Canada. Previous publications include *The Evil Eye of Gondôr*, a play for children, and *'Praying on the Edge'*, ten studies in social issues for home groups. He is currently an international election observer for both the UK government and European Union. Married with two children he has taken early retirement from parish ministry and now writes fulltime. He lives near Glasgow in Scotland.

BY THE SAME AUTHOR

Plays
The Evil Eye of Gondôr

Books
Praying on the Edge

Pamphlet
Albania, Land of Eagles

for more details of Bryan Owen's poetry or to purchase
framed illustrated copies of individual poems
email wordsong.arts@virgin.net

BRYAN OWEN

Blue Daffodils
and other poems

First published by Wordsong Arts
10 Waverley Park, Kirkintilloch
Glasgow G66 2BP Scotland

Matador
9 De Montfort Mews
Leicester LE1 7FW, UK
Tel: (+44) 116 255 9311 / 9312
Email: books@troubador.co.uk
Web: www.troubador.co.uk/matador

ISBN 978-1905886-777

Typeset in 10pt Book Antiqua by Troubador Publishing Ltd, Leicester, UK

Matador is an imprint of Troubador Publishing Ltd

for my son Stuart

Contents

A cold November morning	13
A God-shaped hole	14
Asleep at last	15
Banned books	16
Before the Gates of Heaven	18
Blue daffodils	21
Carpe diem	22
Coffee shop sonnet	23
December lights	24
Deep down things	25
Dilemma	26
Dinner by candlelight	28
Fiji paradise	30
Fiji sunset	32
Forever children	33
Girl in a coffee shop	34
Going to bed	35
I hurt you	36
If you want me	37
In the life before you came	39
Living dangerously	40
Log fires, jazz and good red wine	42
Lonely in time	43
Making decisions	44
Manicured lawns in Chicago	45
Megachurch millionaires	46
Morning hymn	47
Multitasking	48
New day dawning	49
Onions	50

On the shoulders of giants 51
Real words 52
Searching for love 53
Summer storm 54
The afterwards blues 55
The coffee pot 56
The eternal moment 57
The last rose of summer 58
The prostitute 59
The sad clown 60
The Song 61
The tear 62
There was a time 63
Thus do we lose the ones we love 64
Today 65
Triptych for a megachurch 66
Walking into the future 72
We are not descended from fearful men 73
What you do to me 75
Your poem is beautiful 76

Preface

These poems of loving and longing, of hope and excitement, of questioning and uncertainty all arise out of my own peculiar story but are not defined by it. My poetry is the 'poetry of observation' – I watch, take note, consider and reflect on what I see in human behaviour around me.

I wrote my first poems when I was an awkward and very naïve teenager. Out of the pain and trauma of a difficult and loveless childhood I started to explore both the world around me as well as my own inner geography and to do so with words – wonderful, liberating, world-expanding words! I became a teacher of English and for many years immersed myself in other people's words and other people's stories. I taught with passion and commitment a language I loved and a literature that is unsurpassed in its beauty and ability to mirror and reveal the human condition.

But now, in later years, I feel once again the urge to explore my own story and my own perceptions of the people and world around me as I first did all those years ago when, as a teenager, I tentatively began to touch the real world and let it touch me.

Thank you for wanting to share part of this exploration with me. Maybe you will recognize something of yourself or your own ideals in these poems – your own loving and longing, your own hopes and excitement, and your own questioning and doubt as you live through another day and long through another night. And maybe, just maybe, you will smile knowingly from time to time as you read...

Bryan Owen
Glasgow 2007

Blue Daffodils

and other poems

A cold November morning

Colour has been strained
from the day, this slate grey,
cold November morning.
Clouds sit low on the Campsie Fells
and winter trees are silhouetted
against the scudding angry sky.

The whole world is quiet –
even people move
from hearth to heath
in funeral mood.
A lone bird sits atop a pole.
The air is heavy, sombre, leaden
as if all creation were waiting
for the final laboured gasp of the year.

Somewhere, deeply hidden
in the mystery of things,
a shoot is ready to burst
through the heavy, sodden soil.
Meanwhile, we live
in the waiting time
and slowly resist the temptation
to lie down and die.

A God-shaped hole

There's a God-shaped hole
where God should be
and a me-shaped hole
but you can see

there's an emptiness
at the heart of things -
where I should be
there's something missing.

I'm just not there -
I don't know why -
the questions grow
and multiply.

There's a longing in the place
where my heart beats
and a longing in the loins
and a burning heat

that yearns to touch
and satisfy
another's needs
but by and by -

I don't know when
and I don't know how -
I pray to God
to show me now

how the God-shaped hole
gets all filled in
and the 'me' I know
can be me again.

Asleep at last

She is sleeping at last.
Her breasts gently rise and fall
as I trace the line of her lips
(those lips that invited mine!)
and replay in my thoughts
all that we did and said.

She is sleeping at last
(both of us spent!)
but I watch and wait
and hope that when she wakes
she isn't alone
in her bed.

Banned books

'When one burns books one will, in the end, burn people.'
(Heinrich Heine 1797-1856)

'Read banned books,'
says the badge,
'they're your ticket to freedom.'

Banned books, I ask myself?
Are we talking Nazi Germany here
or Communist Russia?
Is this Pol Pot's Cambodia
or Pinochet's Chile
where thoughts are stifled
and books burned
to lifeless, uncreating ash?

No, my friend,
this is America -
that Sweet Land of Liberty
and the Noble Free
whose people proclaim so forcefully
to others their mission
to be the world's sole defender
of precious liberty.

From the mountains to the prairies,
to the oceans, white with foam,
this is America,
liberty's natural home -
a land that's ever bright
with Freedom's holy light
where freedom of opinion
is lauded everywhere in sight.

But... 'I read banned books'
says the button
so all cannot be right.
You can buy one from
any library at all -
(except, of course,
those that ban books).

Thinking our own thoughts,
making our own choices,
voicing our own opinions -
are these the most dangerous
freedoms in the whole world?
Ask the Americans.
They should know.

Before the Gates of Heaven

The line was getting longer
by the minute
but the gates remained firmly shut.
The people looked confused.
Some were holding their rosary beads,
fingering them gently,
offering wordless silent prayers.
Others were standing quietly
looking about them
uncertain what was happening
or what was going to happen
to them.
Two bearded men
nervously played with
their worry beads.

A pastor looked about anxiously
for this was
far beyond his understanding.
Behind him a large group
stood animatedly,
confidently,
bibles in one hand
the other hand raised in
supplication
praising their Lord
and singing.
Some people in the line
were clearly broken
in spirit
and in bodies too,
their hurts etched into
their pained faces.

Just then there seemed to be
a commotion at the back of the line.
An angel was beckoning
to someone
to come forward.

The people looked round
and saw what looked like
an elderly lady
carrying a small bundle.
A young boy held her hand.
He averted his eyes
from the attention of those
in the line
as he shuffled forward
on weary torn feet.
On closer appearance
the elderly lady was not so old
after all
and the small bundle
was that of a child
sucking at her mother's breast
for milk that had dried up days ago.
The pathetic family stumbled forward
guided by the angel
towards the closed gates.

Some of the people in the line
turned away.
Others began to weep.
The little family
had been walking for many days
searching for food to eat,
and water to drink,
and for somewhere safe to live.
The frail beaten boy looked at his mother
and urged her on
just a few steps more.

The great gates slowly opened
and there appeared before the people
the Lord himself.
He watched as the little family drew close
and stood before him.
He touched the mother
and for the first time in many weeks,
many months perhaps,
she stood up straight.

Milk began to flow
and her child began to drink deeply.
The boy looked up
into His face
and returned the Lord's smile.
It was journey's end.

The Lord then looked
at all the people in the line.

'Do you remember,' He said,
'when I told you
that what you did
for the least of these my children
you do it for me?'

And the people nodded
and began to weep.

'My words remain forever true,' He said.
'It is still easier
for a camel to pass through
the eye of a needle
than for those who are rich
to enter the Kingdom of Heaven.'
And with that He turned away
holding the hands
of the woman and her son.
The great gates slowly closed
and there never was heard such a weeping
as was heard before the Gates of Heaven
on that one sad day.

Blue daffodils

I saw blue daffodils
swaying in a lilac breeze
one warm afternoon in May;
a lime-green sun shone down
from a pink-striped sky
as below me
dirty black cars crawled
creepily back to their holes
in the ground.

A bee buzzed brightly,
a cat flew overhead
and it was good to be alive.

Carpe diem

carpe diem, quam minimum credula postero
(pluck the day, and put as little trust as possible in tomorrow)
Horace, Odes I-XI

Seize the pleasures of the moment
make them last more than they may -
treasure all your present glories but
don't count the price you will have to pay.

You don't know what tomorrow will bring
you don't know what Fate has in store -
so pluck the day and seize the moment
but don't trust false promises any more.

Thus spake the cynics in ancient Rome
and ancient Rome should know -
for the gods that failed them on the Tiber
brought their city crashing low.

No price to pay, no fee to find
to guarantee tomorrow -
for fighting wars was what they did
to increase man's share of sorrow.

So strain the wine and keep the feast
for life is brutish brief and short -
there may be no food tomorrow
nor love nor dreams nor girls to court!

They say that youth's a stuff will not endure
so *carpe diem* and don't delay -
kiss your girl and hold her tight
and gather pleasures while ye may.

Coffee shop sonnet

Today I visited some of our special places
where we would oft walk without a care;
I saw all those once familiar faces
yet in my aloneness you were still there.

In the coffee shop's warm and welcoming nooks
I saw again the comforting chair
where you would sit and read your books
but even though empty you were there.

Where we once drank our coffee strong
I struggled with tears in solitary silence;
in the place where we would talk late and long
you are now present by your absence.

My love, I desperately want to explain
so that I can be safe in your arms once again.

December lights

December burns bright!
What hope, what excitement
in this the darkest month of the year.
What a Festival of Light
in homes full of cheer
and such good intent!

While here the Chanukah menorah
burns for eight days of Hebrew joy,
there the Christmas candle
proclaims the birth of a boy
who on that same Temple Mount
heard good Simeon sing
of the light to the Gentiles
this young child would e'er long bring.

In temple and stable
there comes new hope
born of long waiting –
a people unable to cope
with old regrets and past pain
but who long to sing their song once again.

With latkes or turkey,
dreidel or plum pudding,
we celebrate the deep unknown
now become known among us,
and resolve once again
to live by the truths
of the light we see
in every bright window around us.

Deep down things

There are deep down things
of which I cannot speak
but you know what they are
for they inform
my every word and action
and make me
who I am.

There are deep down things
long hidden away
for fear they might be seen
and named
and defeated
but they are waiting silently
hidden in the deep grass
for their opportunity to strike.

These deep down things
these hurts from long ago
these memories quietly strangled
and left slumped somewhere
inside my being
lie dormant
or so I thought.

But there is a perverted resurrection
for every now and again
these deep down things
once thought safely put away
rise up from the dead
somewhere inside my head
and bring me new strife
and the promise of worse to come.

Dilemma

I'm a good boy really -
I take my responsibilities seriously,
I never want to hurt anyone,
I put other people first...
You know who I am -
there are so many like me
in your world,
don't you think?

But I don't want to be good any more -
or, rather, I want to be
both good and bad
at the same time...
You know what I mean?
I'm not so very different
from your friends,
am I?

I want to make love,
I want to play
with those who want to play
and have fun
with those who want me...
You know the kind of thing I mean!
I'm probably not too dissimilar
from yourself,
am I?

But I have a dilemma -
because there is a price to pay
for every joy
and a bill to settle
for every delight...
What I really mean is -
you know the price
and the price is too high,
don't you agree?

So I will remain a good boy -
and be the person
I have to be
for those I love
and for those who love me...
But what I really mean is, well -
there is another side to me
and I rather like it.
Do you know what I mean?
Do you understand?

Dinner by candlelight

Little do they know
what these young lovers do
or who it is who's watching them
and what he has been through;
with their filet mignon medium rare
while gently sipping fine red wine
they've not a worldly care -
these two young lovers as they dine.

Little do they realise
love blind as they now be
that it will all end in tears
you mark my words and see;
I once sat where he sits now
and looked into another's eyes
but now I sip my coffee alone
and bitterly remember how easy love dies.

*

Who is that old guy
sitting over there
looking into his coffee cup
with such a melancholy air?
His sad face edged with icy doom
each furrow a story can tell
but he's casting his wintry gloom
and turning my heaven into hell.

But I have you, my one and only,
and with you all shall be well -
we, of course, shall never be lonely
while we live under Cupid's magic spell.
My thoughts are on one thing alone -
in the hours that lie ahead
I want to hear you moan with joy
when I get you into my bed.

*

I am not so sure of myself
as I look into his eyes
is this what I really want -
living a life of lies?
He wants my body, that I know,
but the spark we once knew has gone -
should I take my leave now
before any great harm is done?

It will break his heart, I know,
but better that than make
what will turn out to be
the most terrible mistake.
I shall tell him now
as he looks into my eyes
that we'll not make our love's vow
but rather say our last goodbyes.

*

Little do they realise
love blind as they now be
that it will all end in tears -
you mark my words and see;
I once sat where he now sits
and looked into her eyes
but now I sip my coffee darkly
and remember when love dies.

Fiji Paradise

They call it Paradise
and for sure
these islands in the sun
are another Eden
producing fruit of every kind
with the seas round about
bringing forth fish after their own kind.

Plates are full
amid the palm trees
and the fiery, sensual hibiscus flowers.
The land is lush,
the lagoons shimmer,
but in this Eden
(as in every Eden, my friend)
there is Adam -
and with his Eve
he brings both a ready smile
and a hidden threat
to all whom he meets.

'Bula!' he cries
in traditional Fijian welcome.
You are welcome indeed
in Paradise
but beneath the warm smile
and behind the friendly hand
Adam watches you
and Cain and Abel -
both sons of the islands -
replay their ancient rivalries
in all the towns and villages of the land.

So there is sorrow and sadness in Paradise...
anger and fear in every village...
but you see none of these things
in the postcards sold
in the tourist hotel.

After all, my friend,
even in Paradise
there are some things
one simply does not speak about.

Fiji Sunset

I watched the sun set
over Savusavu Bay today.
I wanted to write
a poem about it
but words failed me.
I wanted to describe
the oranges and reds
I saw in the sky
but I could not.
I wanted to say a few words
about their brilliance,
their warmth
and the way they made me feel
but I don't think I can.

The sunset was simply
beautiful -
such an inadequate word
for what I saw
in Savusavu Bay
today.

Forever Children

Forever children -
an extra gene here
a missing gene there
a head injury
robbing one of control
another of understanding.

The party was going well -
so many giggles,
shyly holding hands
as other people do
and laughter,
lots of it.
And they danced as best they could
to all the tunes
the rest of us knew
so well.

No malice, no guile, no evil -
we leave all that to the able-minded.
These are the Forever Children
but not knowing they are -
beautiful
but painfully different.

Girl in a coffee shop

She sat at the table
and rummaged in her bag
before sipping her coffee -
black, no sugar.
I watched as she
crossed her long, slender legs,
and then I turned back
to my book
and wished upon a moment...

Going to bed

I love going to bed.
There I cocoon myself
under the covers
and block out the world -
the harsh, hurtful, cruel world -
for yet another long, black and lonely night.

I love the darkness.
I feel the warm, caressing touch of the sheets -
so soothing,
so womb-like and safe.
I unwind, relax
and stretch out
like a contented cat
in front of the fire purring.

But then I reprise the painful day!
The hurtful words
that break my heart
and tear my soul
repeat themselves.
The old tapes play
and I remember
all those dark moments
I'd rather forget
and send away.

So even in my bed,
my friend,
when I am alone
in the darkness
and the warmth
I realise I am not alone at all
or ever will be.

I hurt you

I hurt you.
I wasn't thinking
except about myself.
Words, once said,
can never be taken back –
I realise that now.
Is it too late?
Only you can tell me
whether you love me still.
Can we talk?

If you want me

If you want me
win me -
I am not so very far away,
my love.

If you want me
woo me -
I am waiting for
your call.

We have drifted apart, my love,
and we don't speak as once we did;
the future seems bleak
and you are afraid -
I see it in your eyes.

But you blame me
for something
that belongs to us both:
you are not the fixed point
and I am not the rudderless vessel
in our broken love.

But if you want me
try again -
but that is the problem,
isn't it?
You are too afraid.

Is it pride?
Or a fear of rejection, perhaps?
Or are you simply unwilling
to open yourself
to the possibility
of rediscovered love
and all the pain
that comes with it?

If you want me
win me,
woo me.
I am not so very far away,
not so very far at all...

In the life before you came

In the life before you came
  and turned my world upside down
I knew what to do with my raw days.
In my freedom to be I was alone
  but safe in the rime of my aloneness.

But then you came through my door.
You brought with you such passion,
  such humour, joy and intense love,
  it was as if I were reborn.

How, then, can I go back
  to what I knew without you?
How do I go back to those chilly dark days
  before your smile and touch
  and the beguiling comfort of your voice
  lit my fire and scarred me forever?

Living Dangerously

Some people live very dangerously indeed.
They jump out of small planes,
they swim with great sharks
and they climb the world's highest mountains.
These things are truly dangerous
I think you would agree.

But when I live dangerously
(and I do)
it means being with people,
flesh and blood people,
red-faced sweaty people,
and people weighed down
with heavy memories -
memories that hurt.

It means getting to know them
and letting them touch me -
not in the physical sense
you understand
(although I would like that very much)

but dropping my guard,
liking them
and loving them,
and being liked and loved in return.

That really is such hard work.
Liking people
takes more courage than jumping out of planes
or swimming with sharks.
And it's so very, very dangerous,
don't you agree?

Sometimes I like to break out of the old routines -
to live outside the box
(as some people say),
to be unconventional,
take risks
and try something new.

But that's so very, very dangerous
I think you would agree...
for it means that perhaps the most dangerous person
in all the wide world
is me?

Log fires, jazz and good red wine

But you cried!
I saw your tears!
There is a vulnerable side to you, my love
and I don't want to hurt you.
I am vulnerable too but hey -
that is what makes me *me*!

This is the point where you and I
should be sitting on the sofa
looking into the flames of the log fire -
music playing softly
(some midnight jazz, I think)
and a glass of red wine in our hands
(full-bodied, rich with a glorious after-taste).

This is the time for just 'being', don't you think?
You can talk and talk
but there always comes a moment
when the talking stops... a moment
when you sit quietly
and enjoy the silence together.
These are the most special of times -
the times when no words are necessary.

And this is just such a time -
the two of us sitting peacefully
each wondering what's going through the other's mind
each hoping the other is not hurting too much.

And this is our time -
watching the flames dance in the log fire
holding a glass of good red wine
and listening to sad notes
drifting in the still evening air...

Lonely in time

Surrounded by people
  surging around me
submerged by activity
  demanding my time

chasing the diary
  I'm running to keep up
I've too much to do
  but not enough time

I'm busy and tired
  I need someone to turn to
a friend of my own
  to give me some time

someone to pour out
  my troubles and cares to
a friend and a lover
  to give me their time.

I've told you my story
  so what will you do?
I need someone special -
  and wish it were you...

Making decisions

Sometimes I feel like
one of those cartoon characters
with an angel on one shoulder
and a devil on the other.

The angel is whispering one thing
and the devil something else
and both sound right
or, at the least,
very, very desirable.

Manicured lawns in Chicago

Manicured lawns
surround immaculate houses,
well-behaved trees
sway gently in the breeze.

A pristine fountain
sprays clear cool water
and the laughing stream
runs sparkling into the idyllic pond.

Four geese fly
in a neat skein overhead
as impeccably coloured flowers
turn their obedient heads towards the sun.

Behind each newly painted door...
inside each unsoiled spic-and-span home...
perfect people
live perfect lives

while outside
this gated paradise
real people
live and move and have their being.

Megachurch millionaires

I went to church the other day
feeling the need as one does to pray.
With twenty thousand other good people
praising the Lord beneath that steeple
I realised what a very heavy load it was
to keep that show on the road.

Over five hundred paid workers
shouldered the people's cares
but only the church's pastors
became millionaires.

Morning hymn

I sat on the old wooden veranda
early one gentle island morning.
Heavy rain had awoken me
but the night's sticky air had cleared
with the rising of the sun.

I sat watching the waves
crashing on the reef not far distant
as they had been doing
for thousands of years
before men wondered why.

The dark, heavy rain clouds slowly thinned
and as the light of a new day strengthened
God used all the colours in the Divine palette
to paint the sky
in lighter shades of glory.

A fruit bat flew home to roost -
her night's work done.
A silver dew covered the grass
as the mynah bird sang her morning song.
I sat entranced
at the start of this perfect new day
and thanked God I was alive.

Multitasking

'It's amazing that women can juggle 95 things at the same time
while men make such a big deal out of just one or two!'
I laughed out loud when she said that
as I continued cooking the dinner.

'Don't go there,' I said,
holding the phone with one hand
while whisking an omelette with the other.
I looked at the laundry in the basket
and thought
I really should do something about it.

The call ended I looked in the cupboard
and made a mental note
of all that was missing
while composing in another part of my head
an email I had to write
(quite a serious issue
needing my professional input, you understand).
Mind you, the carpets still needed vacuuming,
there were biscuit crumbs on the settee
and there was that presentation I still had to complete.

Okay! The omelette's done -
I'll call the kids.

Nobody told me that being a single dad
could be so much fun.
After a cup of coffee I will save the world.

New day dawning

Through the ice curtain
of slowly curling cloud
a hint of morning light
promises untried possibilities:
once again,
as for a thousand
times ten thousand years,
creation is re-created
out of night's dark Sabbath rest.

Yes! I will live this perfect moment
as if it were my last
or my first.
I breathe deeply
and taste the crisp morning air:
I'm suddenly thankful
for this one new day
and another chance to be.

Onions

She said I'm like an onion –
I had so many hidden layers.
I told her that
if she stopped peeling
she wouldn't cry so much.

On the shoulders of giants

(for religious fundamentalists everywhere…)

When Plato engaged in Dialogue
and Aristotle pondered the Cosmos,
when the Buddha sat under his Tree
and Jesus taught in Galilee,

when Newton framed his Laws
and Einstein had relatively more Time,
when Darwin boarded the Beagle
and Watson and Crick mapped our DNA,

when Ulugh Beg observed the Stars
and the Ancients discovered Zero,
when Shakespeare filled the Great O
and Tolstoy scaled the Heights,

when Gandhi destroyed an Empire
and Martin Luther King had a Dream,
when Schubert tickled his Trout
and Beethoven lit up our hearts with Joy

who would have thought
that on the shoulders of giants like these
and of all the giants who have led the way
from the caves of fear and ignorance of long ago

weak men (for they are usually men) -
creating a God in their own sad and angry image -
would destroy all the giants we have ever known
and make us all become small again?

Real words

Have you thought about
the coldness of words
when you can't hear them
being delivered?

Have you thought of
your friend speaking them
but you not wanting to
hear them?

He is such a long way away
but is as close as your fingertips
and the screen you watch
night after night.

A new whisper, a new message,
another reply
and cyberspace buzzes
with words that are not words.

Tell me when you're thirsty!
Tell me when you'd like a drink!
Then you can hear my words for real -
the ones that have sounds and meaning attached to them.

Real words can't be deleted -
they can't be re-written or amended -
so they are quite dangerous, I think,
and full of intent.

Real words, of course, come attached
to a person made of flesh and blood;
real words don't appear on a screen
only to be wiped off again at your convenience.
So here I am
with so many words to give you -
and there you are, safe and sound,
alone in your room with the screen blinking.

Searching for love

I've been searching for love
all my days -
yearning and aching,
longing to belong,
to be wanted in the wanting.

I looked for love the wide world over -
I listened to wise men's words
and women who whispered they knew.

Then one day, unexpectedly,
I found the end to all my searching -
in your glance, your touch, your smile,
the hug you gave me
and the warm caressing words
you showered upon me.

In that singular moment
all was well
and all will be well
for what I had sought
these many long years
I had already known in you
and missed in the searching.

Summer Storm

Distant thunder mumbles and rumbles across the sky
like a slow belch gathering force from somewhere
deep down below.
We read the signs
and take cover.

Heavy grey cloud
tinged with the remains of sunshine
slowly fills all the sky.
The world darkens menacingly.
Distant mountains disappear.
Earth and cloud touch in holy communion
somewhere beyond the pine forest.

Trees dance in the wind
and leaves twitter and rustle
in expectation.
They, too, know what is to come.
Chipmunks and groundhogs
hide somewhere safe and warm -
and wait.

Suddenly it is cold.
The time has come.
We are ready.

The afterwards blues

Why, dear friend, are we blessed
with desire?

What persuaded the gods
that a glimpse
a mere hint
a scintilla
of that which is forbidden
beyond reach
untouchable
should so turn our minds
that we are prepared to risk
all that we are and
all that we have
for that one moment of supreme pleasure?

It is all illusion, my friend.
We know the promise
is rarely ever fulfilled.
We are never fully satisfied.

Yet we continue to be
bedazzled
beguiled
seduced
by a glimpse
a thought
and a hope.

And I don't suppose we would want it
any other way.

The coffee pot

She brought the coffee pot to the table and poured.
We sat facing one another
in the kitchen of her days.
I took the mug and warmed my hands
as her knowing eyes met my gaze.
The hot coffee steamed right into my mind
while I tried thoughts and feelings and words to find.
'Let's talk,' she said
and I wove my thread –
and the coffee pot heard
    every
        beautiful
            word.

The eternal moment

We stood facing one another
in the doorway of maybe -
the moment a beat longer
than it might have been.

I wanted to touch your cheek
to run my finger slowly across your lips -
to touch your precious words
and tell you mine.

I would have unbuttoned
the blouse of your mind
but fear bade me 'No'.

Your tear-touched eyes
were open to possibilities and desire.
For an eternal moment
I lost myself in them -
but I blinked
and suddenly you were gone.

Will I find you again?
I know you are there.
Are you watching for me, I wonder -
enduring the pleasure of aching -
hoping I will find you again?

I want you and the comfort of you -
and I crave once more
the promise of perfect moments
in all the touching yet to come.

The last rose of summer

The last rose of summer
leaned into the chill autumnal wind
and wept a tear of morning dew.
It was time.

The garden was growing empty.
The butterflies had already gone,
a few lazy wasps flew drunkenly
among the bare branches,
the last of the honey bees
were gathering what nectar they could.

The last rose of summer
knew it was time to let go
but even as its petals fluttered
slowly to the ground
and danced in the skittering wind

the rose knew that
somewhere beyond the cold
a new spring was already preparing
to visit once again
a sadly dying and cold world.

The Prostitute

'Would you like some company, mister?
Can I come with you?
We could have some fun, mister.
Please…'

She was beautiful -
olive-skinned,
long-legged,
small breasted
with inviting lips
and sensual fingers
touching mine
as I walked the street
under dulled lamps.

But inside -
in places where I could not see -
her beauty had been spoiled,
despoiled,
in ways I cannot know
or ever understand.

How can I know her hurts?
Her lifeless eyes remind me
that for her
there is no redemption.
Her pimp sees to that.

The sad clown

The sad clown
sits down at his table.
He rubs some cream on here
and draws some bold lines there.
He puts on a big red nose
and wonderfully funny clothes,
and the people laugh
and feel much better for
having watched the clown
fall down.

I put on my clothes this morning –
priestly vestments that set me apart
to speak from the heart
about the Great Spirit we call God.
I spoke to the people
and gave them bread and wine.
Afterwards there were
warm smiles and firm handshakes.
They were a sign
that I genuinely cared
as they told me of
their worries and ills
and all the other concerns
they kindly shared.

Then I went to my room
and took off my special clothes,
my make-up,
my funny red nose.
And like Jesus of old
at the tomb of his friend
I recognised a dying
I couldn't accept.
Something had come to an end
and I stood there and wept.

The Song

In the beginning was the Word -
then there two words
then many, many, many words
until there was a cacophony,
a babel,
of angry, vicious sounds
reaching for the sky
drowning out the first Word -
the one that was spoken in the beginning.

Those who shouted the loudest
received the most,
behaved the worst
and they thought their words
the most important words
ever spoken.

But all these words
and every word
will disappear into silence -
they will not last
nor will those who speak them
for their inconsequential fiefdoms
are built on air
and are as insubstantial
as a will o' the wisp -
and just as thinly unimportant.

So at the ending of all things
will still be the Word -
and that Word
will outlast all our other words -
and it will be a song of love
as it has always been,
the most beautiful song ever sung,
and it will be sung for me
and for any who will listen
for ever and for ever.

The Tear

The tear rolled down her face
but was quickly wiped away
(as tears often are)
leaving no trace of its journey.
Suddenly there was no beginning
and no ending.
The tear didn't exist.

Would that its cause
could be as quickly
wiped away
and the beating, hurting heart
left clean and dry.

There was a time

There was a time
when we would spend our evenings together
talking, laughing, listening to music
and one another
with a glass of wine or three
and soft lighting to complement
the dreamy cushions we lie on.
I would stroke your hair,
you would touch my lips
and our hearts would race wildly
with the excitement of it all.

Now things are different.
When evening comes we are too tired for pleasure -
older now we irritate one another beyond measure.
You do some chores,
the children make a noise
and a thousand tempestuous demands
while I escape to another meeting
anywhere beyond our doors.

Soon things will change though!
Once more we shall spend our evenings together
talking, forgetting, reminiscing
over a cup of tea (just one, not three)
with walking sticks to help us
out of the hard chairs we sit on.
You will rub my back,
I will find your meds
and our hearts will race wildly
with the exhaustion of it all.

What did we lose in the living?
And why didn't we see it coming?

Thus do we lose the ones we love

I poured some wine
  but it was left untouched;
I prepared a feast
  but it was left uneaten;
I bought a gift
  but it sat there unopened.

I said let's go out together
  but I went alone;
I said let's stay at home
  but I sat by myself;
I said let's walk by the tumbling river
  or through the rolling green hills
  but as ever I walked in solitude
  with only my own thoughts for company

for my love said to me,
'I have bought a field
and five yoke of oxen
and have married a busy life:
please excuse me for
I cannot come.'

Thus do we lose the ones we love -
  not with a bang or a whimper
but from a thousand slices of bitter sadness
  and an overwhelming cup of sorrow.

Today

Today is going to be an adventure -
I've not been here before.

Yesterday is over:
I can't change what I did or said
no matter how much I try.
Life is too short for regrets.
On the other hand
tomorrow hasn't arrived
but it will come when the time is right
without any help from me.

Today, then, is all I have:
and I can choose
whether to enjoy it or damn it,
to engage with it or withdraw from it.
Today I can choose
to smile or cry,
to love or hate
to build up or break down.

I know that today
some things will happen that are planned
but I also know
there will be a few surprises as well.
Whatever comes along
I will be strong,
I will be positive
and I will make this
the best day it can possibly be –
for you, my love, and for me.

Triptych for a Megachurch

I

They came in their thousands
that one fall night -
their full cars
filling the lot
and the lot
filling the world.

The shuttle bus
gathered them up
as a hen gathers her chicks -
these spiritual shoppers
out for a good evening
looking for the bargain
of their souls.

They settled themselves
into comfortable seats
in a purpose driven auditorium
of purpose driven proportions
having already quenched their thirst
with a coffee
or a soda
or perhaps something a little more
substantial
bought in the manna blessed restaurant
conveniently situated nearby.

Some had wandered through
the bookshop
on the upper level
looking for easy reading
and easier answers
to help them face
the wretched complications
of the world they lived in
but from which by faith and choice
and godless fear
they were set apart.

So with purchases in hand
and well-thumbed bibles too
these haggardly anxious penitents
waited in their seats,
sitting comfortably enough,
chatting amiably
while reading the ads
on the television screens
urging them to register
for the next special meeting.

Then suddenly
the lights dimmed
and the band began to play.
The show was about to begin...

II

He spoke
for nearly an hour -
this pastor.

The band had performed
their songs
newly written for the occasion
but just as newly forgotten
and in between
the girl had
spoken her words
of praise -
and all the people
said 'Amen'.

Then the supplicants gathered their thoughts
as the offering was taken
and a prayer was said;
they readied themselves

to hear the words of unknowing
they had come to expect
from their wonderfully anointed pastor
and chief executive.
Formerly with a hi-tech company
somewhere far away
they were so blessed
he had deigned to come to this place
and to these people
bringing his hi-tech skills,
his folksy words of insight
and kindly fatherly oversight.
His focus, of course, was on the family -
all rocking chairs and apple pie -
his church was filled with glorifying praise
most of it to God on high.

As he talked and joshed
in the all-American way
his key points
helpfully
appeared on the television screens before them
so that every word he said
would be gathered up
and nothing
might be lost.

The jokes were carefully
placed
and the people laughed
as they were meant to do.
He was their friend -
this man they might not
ever meet,
whose names he would never know,
but whose shoelaces
they were unworthy even to untie -
but they could buy his books
helpfully
made available after the service
on tables near the doors.

This act of worship
was for the more advanced members
of the fellowship.
The pastor offered in-depth teaching
and the people made many
soul-saving notes
so their bibles would at last make
sense
and they swooned in admiration
for this was a good man
speaking good words
with which they all agreed.

The television cameras
(how helpful they were)
showed his smile
on the screens.
His earnest imprecations
cut everyone to the quick
and the people warmed to his
knowing winks
for they knew
that although he was far away
and very small
television made him appear
so much closer
and more real than you would think.

And then it was all over.
He raised his hand in benediction
because he loves the church
with a very great love.
And the people loved him back
and warmly applauded
to tell him so.

Then suddenly he was gone.

III

I sat for a while
in my comfortable seat

in this awesome theatre of dreams.
The other people in my row
pushed past me
anxious to put into practice
all the pastor had taught them.
I opened my mouth to say goodbye
but they hurried away
and without speaking
I watched them go.

Friendly volunteers were everywhere
giving freely of their time
and their smiles
(and their uniforms helpfully setting them apart)
walkie-talkies in hand
taking instructions from someone
unseen but all-seeing,
directing the people,
ensuring everything
ran smoothly
and without trouble,
and that no one was uncertain or
lost.

I thought for a moment
I might buy a slice of pizza
and a root beer
to end this most perfect of evenings
but there were so many others in line
whose needs were far greater than mine.
I turned away
and momentarily dismissed the emptiness
I felt in my stomach.

For a while I wandered round the atrium
browsing the books
all the church's many pastors
had so generously written.
I read the power-designed notices
advertising all the church's power-filled meetings:
there were so many programs
to register for but

helpfully
there were generous discounts
for those who had been saved.

The crowds outside the auditorium
began to thin
as people caught the buses
back to the parking lots.
Some quietly strolled
beneath the willow trees
or alongside the specially manicured creek.
Under the stars,
beneath the mystery of it all,
the people knew how much
they were needed in this place
and even on this one fall night
they looked forward to their next coming.

Satisfied and comforted
in body and soul,
they drove off
into the night
their tail-lights
glowing red
in the darkness
of it all.

Walking into the future

I'm walking into the future
backwards;
I don't really know
where I'm going
although I do know
where I would like to end up.

I'm walking into the future
backwards;
I know
where I've been
and I know all too well
what I've done in times past

and the past with all its mistakes
must be my guide
for without remembering it
how can I know
how to walk into the future
at all?

We are not descended from fearful men

(in memory of Edward R. Murrow, American journalist, 1908-1965)

We are not descended from fearful men,
my friend,
yet (fearful fools that we are)
we still fail to confront
the tyrannies of evil men

who by ruthless use of money
or force of twisted personality
or rapacious lust for power
would imprison us all

so that they might become God
and we their worshippers
obediently bowing down
and giving them the glory
in eternal Faustian submission.

They are little men with big bibles
who focus on other people's families
and other people's bedrooms...

They are little men with big cheque books
who know the cost of everything
but the value of nothing...

They are little men with big guns
who at the push of a button orgasm
at their phallic missiles of shock and awe...

They are, my friend, little men with big promises
who betray the trust of voters
for a mess of potage at the tables of power.

Where are the truly big men, my friend,
who by their simple deeds

can move millions to love
and who with a simple word
can restore our sense of self-worth?

Where are the big men, my friend,
who have nowhere to lay their own head
nor would they want to
while millions have no bed
to call their own?

And where am I, my friend,
and what is my part
in these things?

Who will show me the way
in which I should go
or should I merely say
good night and good luck
and hope for the best...?

What you do to me

You take my words
and make them mean
something unintended.

You take my heart
and break it so
when all our love seems ended.

You take my life
and turn it round
and leave me quite offended.

You call again
I hold you tight
our arguments transcended.

Your poem is beautiful

Your poem is beautiful
but I can't wait for the day
when you send me one
full of happiness and joy.

Your thoughts are tender
but I long for the hour
when you tell me
how much you love me.

Your hands are slender
but I ache for the moment
when you touch me, caress me
and hold me close.

Your face is comely
but I can't wait for the day
when it lights up the world
and makes me zing with delight.

Your voice is sensual
but I yearn to hear you sing
the song of our love
and the life of our days.

But your eyes are rheumy
and through the tears
I see the pain
that is eating away at your soul.

You are you, *mi amor*,
and I love you as you are -
your poem is beautiful
and tells me all I need to know.

if you have enjoyed these poems
Bryan Owen's next collection

Kokopelli's dance

will be published in late 2007
full details from Wordsong Arts
Kirkintilloch G66 2BP Scotland
email: wordsong.arts@virgin.net

Printed in the United Kingdom
by Lightning Source UK Ltd.
119857UK00001BA/1-6